Dear Parent:

Congratulations! Your child is taking the first steps on an exciting journey. The destination? Independent reading!

STEP INTO READING® will help your child get there. The program offers five steps to reading success. Each step includes fun stories and colorful art. There are also Step into Reading Sticker Books, Step into Reading Math Readers, Step into Reading Write-In Readers, Step into Reading Phonics Readers, and Step into Reading Phonics First Steps! Boxed Sets—a complete literacy program with something for every child.

Learning to Read, Step by Step!

Ready to Read Preschool–Kindergarten
• big type and easy words • rhyme and rhythm • picture clues
For children who know the alphabet and are eager to begin reading.

Reading with Help Preschool–Grade 1
• basic vocabulary • short sentences • simple stories
For children who recognize familiar words and sound out new words with help.

Reading on Your Own Grades 1–3
• engaging characters • easy-to-follow plots • popular topics
For children who are ready to read on their own.

Reading Paragraphs Grades 2–3
• challenging vocabulary • short paragraphs • exciting stories
For newly independent readers who read simple sentences with confidence.

Ready for Chapters Grades 2–4
• chapters • longer paragraphs • full-color art
For children who want to take the plunge into chapter books but still like colorful pictures.

STEP INTO READING® is designed to give every child a successful reading experience. The grade levels are only guides. Children can progress through the steps at their own speed, developing confidence in their reading, no matter what their grade.

Remember, a lifetime love of reading starts with a single step!

Dactyls! *is dedicated to the great museum at Central Park West and 79th Street, in New York City. That's where I saw my first dactyl.*
—Dr. Bob

The author and editor would like to thank Dr. Joanna Wright for her assistance in the preparation of this book.

Text copyright © 2005 by Dr. Robert T. Bakker.
Illustrations copyright © 2005 by Luis V. Rey.
All rights reserved under International and Pan-American Copyright Conventions. Published in the United States by Random House Children's Books, a division of Random House, Inc., New York, and simultaneously in Canada by Random House of Canada Limited, Toronto.

www.stepintoreading.com

Educators and librarians, for a variety of teaching tools, visit us at
www.randomhouse.com/teachers

Library of Congress Cataloging-in-Publication Data
Bakker, Robert T.
Dactyls! : dragons of the air / by Robert T. Bakker ; illustrated by Luis V. Rey.
    p. cm. — (Step into reading. Step 4)
ISBN 0-375-83013-8 (trade) — ISBN 0-375-93013-2 (lib. bdg.)
1. Pterodactyls—Juvenile literature. I. Rey, Luis V. II. Title. III. Series.
QE862.P7B35 2005   567.918—dc22   2004007482

Printed in the United States of America   First Edition   10 9 8 7 6 5 4 3 2 1

STEP INTO READING, RANDOM HOUSE, and the Random House colophon are registered trademarks of Random House, Inc.

DACTYLS!
DRAGONS OF THE AIR

by Dr. Robert T. Bakker
illustrated by Luis V. Rey

Random House New York

Chapter One

I dig fossil bones. That's my job. My crew digs in the rocks in the Cowboy State— Wyoming. We excavate giant bones from long-necked brachiosaurs, armor-plated stegosaurs, and meat-eating allosaurs, who had steak-knife teeth.

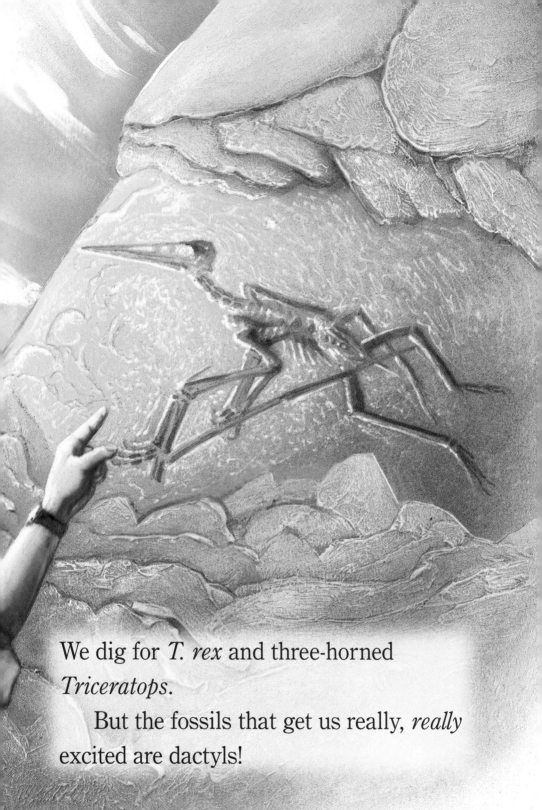

We dig for *T. rex* and three-horned
Triceratops.
 But the fossils that get us really, *really*
excited are dactyls!

We call them "flying dragons." Their scientific name is *pterosaur*. But whatever you call them, they are simply wonderful!

Dactyls came in all sizes. The biggest were fifty feet from wing tip to wing tip. That's *much* bigger than the biggest flying bird today, the California condor. Dactyl giants were so strong they could pick up an average-sized third-grade girl and fly away!

But there were tiny dactyls, too. German scientists have found dactyls as small as robins. If they were alive today, one of those dactyls could fit inside a parakeet cage.

I'll introduce you to the dactyl my crew just discovered. No, I didn't find it. A middle school teacher did—Mr. Ed Pulver from Kokomo, Indiana. Ed is one of our best diggers.

Chapter Two

Imagine a hot, hot day in Wyoming
144 million years ago. The landscape is
flat, *flat*, FLAT! The mountains you see
today don't exist. A huge swampy lake is
buzzing with big Jurassic bugs.

You see a huge dinosaur. It's an
apatosaur, nearly a hundred feet long. He's
looking for some fresh green leaves to eat.
He stops to stare at three
little fish with shiny scales.

Fffffwoooooop! Splash! Zippity-zip!
Something snatches a fish and carries it up into the sky.

What was *that*? the apatosaur asks himself without using words. (Apatosaurs had very small brains.) He looks around.

Forty feet above the water, the apatosaur sees a stunning sight. Beautiful white wings, curved backward, soar in graceful circles. The flying creature looks down with her big, clear blue eyes.

She's carrying a fish in her long jaws—and it's still flopping around.

Crunch! Crunch! She bites down hard with her sharp teeth. *Gulp!* The winged white dragon swallows the fish headfirst.

A second fish-eating flier arrives. He has bright red eyes. He watches the water. And watches . . . and watches . . .

Fwoop! He swoops down—fast!

Zoom! He zips over the water and dips his bill. His teeth snag a slippery fish. And then—*zip*—up he flies.

The two dactyls are happy. They fly around each other. And then they land on a thick branch of an old dead tree. They scramble around on all fours.

Loud peeps come from a hole in the wood. Five gawky dactyl chicks poke out their heads and open their mouths. *Glurk-glurk.* The female dactyl regurgitates her fish—she brings it back up her throat. Then the chick gobbles down the fishy morsel.

Don't say "Yuck! Gross!" Lots of animals regurgitate. Wolves feed their young that way. So do hawks and eagles. The food comes up all nice and warm and yummy.

Chapter Three

We call our Wyoming dactyl "Snaggle-Tooth" because it has big, sharp-edged teeth that curve back like a meat-eating dinosaur's. That's unusual. Most dactyl teeth are straight. Some slant forward so the dactyl can stab squid with a quick downstroke of its head into the water. And some giant dactyls didn't have any teeth at all. They used their sharp beaks to spear prey.

Snaggle-Tooth has a famous relative—*Pterodactylus*. *Pterodactylus* hunted in Jurassic oceans in Germany. But our Wyoming dactyl hunted over lakes and swamps. How can we tell lake dactyls from ocean dactyls?

Easy. Squid and clams. Squid live *only* in salt water. And squid-type fossils are often found with *Pterodactylus* in Germany. In Wyoming, we find our Snaggle-Tooth dactyl alongside special clam fossils. Today these clams live *only* in freshwater lakes. So if you want to be a dactyl paleontologist, you've got to know your mollusks—that's the name for clams and squid (and snails and octopuses, too).

Dactyl bones are amazing—they're hollow! Instead of being solid like most other skeletons, dactyl bones are like straws made from bone. Even the skull bones are hollow. Dactyls were flying "airheads"!

Hollow bones enabled dactyls to fly and dive and zoom. When they were alive, dactyls had air tubes that connected all the bones. And the tubes were connected to big air chambers in the chest and tummy. Air was everywhere inside and moving through the tubes and chambers all the time.

That's why dactyls could fly.

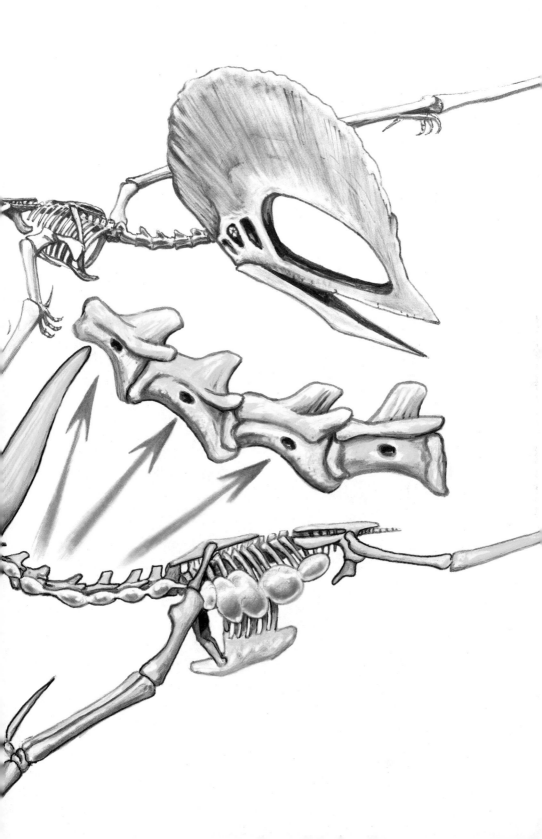

Today the only animals with air tubes are birds. The air moving inside lets the bird breathe better than you or I. Birds can fly at 35,000 feet, where the air is thin. Our human lungs aren't nearly that good. We start gasping at 14,000 feet, and we pass out at 20,000 feet.

Chapter Four

The first scientist to think about dactyls seriously was the Reverend William Buckland in England, way back in the 1820s. (Surprise! Many early bone-diggers were ministers.) Fossil scientists think by drawing pictures. Buckland made doodles of his dactyls. Oodles of doodles.

Buckland's doodles showed dactyls hopping around like bats—vampire bats who have long legs and run fast on all four feet.

Much later, in the 1970s, some scientists said Buckland was wrong. They said dactyls walked like birds, on their hind legs. Who was right? Scientists like to argue. That's good. It gets everybody to dig up more dactyl data. In the 1980s, my friend Dr. Martin Lockley found really good fossil footprints—lots of 'em—made by dactyls. The tracks looked like vampire bat footprints.

The Reverend Buckland's doodles were right, after all!

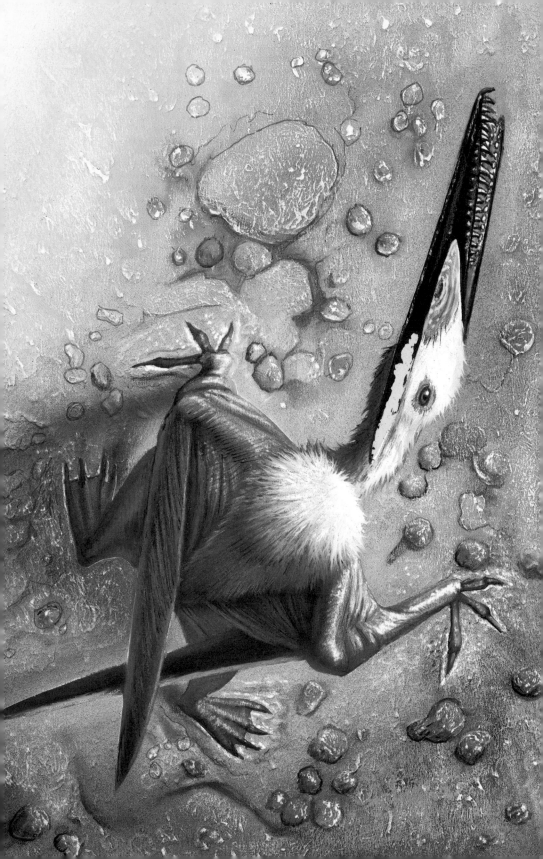

Buckland's pictures of dactyls make them look dark and scary. Like bats. But I think he was wrong about the "dark" part. Bats have to be dark because they fly at night. Dactyls were relatives of birds, and most birds fly in daylight.

Birds that fly over oceans and lakes are often white—that's so fish can't see the birds overhead in the light, bright sky. Most dactyl bones are dug from ancient oceans and lakes, so when you draw a dactyl, use a lot of white.

Save your colored pencils for the dactyl head. Puffins are seabirds that have bills colored yellow, orange, and black. Buckland's favorite dactyl—a medium-sized critter called *Dimorphodon*—had a tall, pinched bill just like a puffin's. So I think *Dimorphodon* had bright colors, too.

Chapter Five

Jurassic dactyls were mostly small. In the next period, the Cretaceous, dactyls became real giants. These super-dactyls grew weird crests of bone that went up and back over their foreheads. Or up over their bills. Male dactyls usually had the bigger crest. Today male and female birds often have different colors—the male is usually more brightly colored. Dactyls were probably like that, too.

There's one big dactyl from Argentina that was a shocking-pink color all over. *Maybe.* Its teeth were ultra-thin and crowded together, so they made a sieve for catching tiny lake shrimp. Flamingos feed that way. Flamingos are pink because they eat shrimp that eat pink-colored algae. And the pink dye gets into their feathers.

The Argentine dactyl must have fed the same way—and it might have turned pink!

What kind of skin did dactyls have? Fossilized impressions of dactyl skin show short, hairlike things all over. A live dactyl would feel soft, like a hamster.

And dactyls would feel *warm*! Many scientists used to say that dactyls were cold-blooded reptiles, like lizards. (Another word for dactyl is *pterosaur,* which means "winged lizard.") Lizards get cold on cloudy days because they need the sun to heat themselves up.

But the Reverend Buckland didn't think his dactyls were cold-blooded lizards. He thought dactyls were more like warm-blooded birds. And today most paleontologists agree. Dactyl lungs worked so hard that the body was kept warm all the time.

I'd love to have a tame *Dimorphodon*. I'd teach it to catch trout for me in Wyoming lakes. At night I'd let it curl up on my bed.

Dactyls weren't just warmer than lizards, they were smarter, too. X-rays of fossil skulls show that the space for the brain is big—much bigger than a lizard's. A pet *Pterodactylus* might be smart enough to learn games—maybe something like "fetch the flying Frisbee."

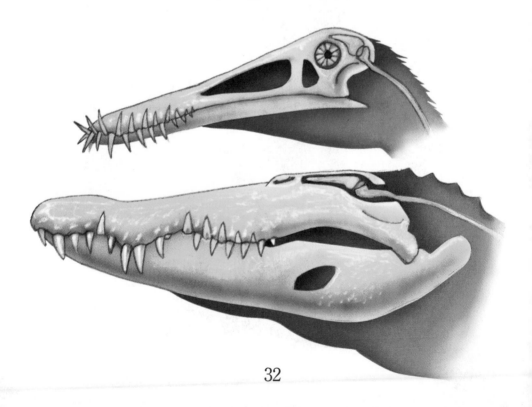

Chapter Six

Old books say dactyl wings were weak because the wing skin was soft and flabby. Wrong! German and Russian fossils dug in the 1970s show that the wings were made strong by special rods in the skin. Plus, dactyls used special joints to control the wing.

Look at *Dimorphodon*'s hand. It's weird. Three skinny little fingers have sharp, hooked claws. Those were for climbing. One more finger holds the front edge of the wing. But this wing-finger is thicker and stronger than the thigh! It's so strong it could flap the wing and make the dactyl take off.

All dactyl hands had something no other critter in the world has—a bone spike for expert flight. The spike swiveled around and pulled the front edge of the wing up or down. In an airplane, that's called a "leading-edge flap." It lets the pilot maneuver at slow speed.

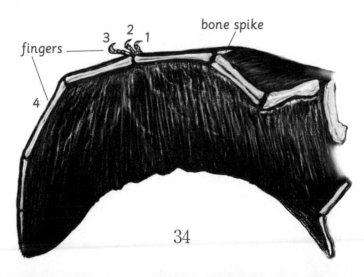

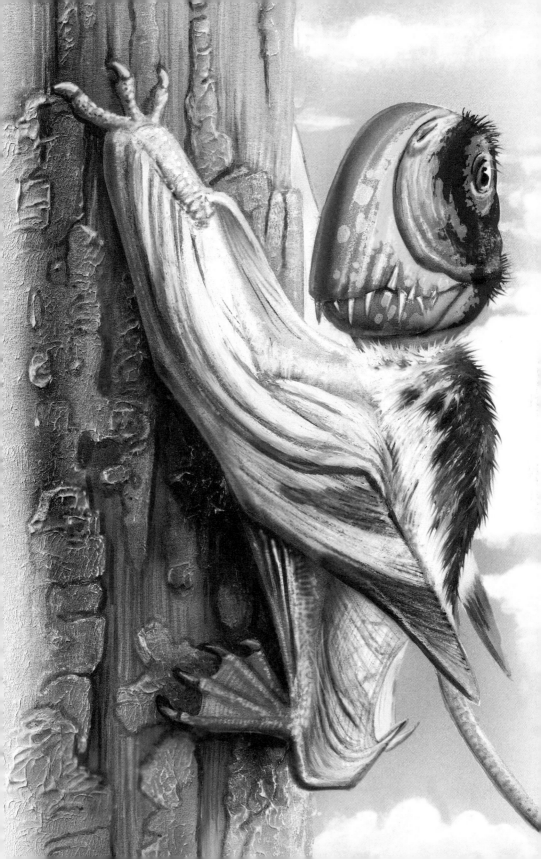

At the back of the wing, *Dimorphodon* has special wing joints, too. There's a swivel on the pinkie toe, so the hind leg and tail could steer the wing, like a bat.

Dimorphodon has yet another way to steer—a rudder way at the end of the tail. This dactyl had so many ways to steer, it could turn and bank and dive and climb.

Dimorphodon was big for a long-tailed dactyl—as big as a seagull. All the super-giants were almost tailless and they didn't have a swivel on their pinkie toe. Little *Pterodactylus* was built that way, too. But these short-tailed dactyls had extra-strong wing-fingers, so they were super fliers.

The giants soared on updrafts—air currents that rise where hot beach meets cold water. *Pterodactylus* could zip around the sea air.

What would dactyls taste like? Turkey! Wild turkey! Dactyl breastbones were big, so the flight muscles were thick and meaty. You could cook a big dactyl for Thanksgiving. *Titanopteryx* would weigh over a hundred pounds cooked with stuffing. That's enough to feed a family of fifty, plus leftovers for dactyl sandwiches and soup!

My favorite big dactyls were dive-bombers. *Pteranodon* had a beak shaped like a pelican's. And extra joints to keep its neck from being twisted. Some pelicans today dive straight into the water to grab fish. Whole groups of pelicans dive-bomb together and catch entire schools of fish. *Pteranodon* could probably do that, too.

Imagine that you are a mackerel-sized fish in the Cretaceous Period and you are swimming along with your mackerel-like family. What's your worst mackerel nightmare? (Actually, fish brains are too small to dream, so they can't have nightmares. But you know what I mean.)

A squadron of *Pteranodon* dive-bombers! You wouldn't see them coming. The white wings and bodies would be invisible if you looked up into the bright sky. You'd have no warning. Then . . .

KER-SPLOSH!! A two-foot-long beak crashes into the water above. You thrash your tail fin to get out of the way . . . but it's too late. *Pteranodon* probably had a pelican-style pouch on its jaws, so it wouldn't even have to touch you to catch you. All it would have to do was to expand the pouch underwater and in you'd go. *Glurk!*

Then *splosh . . . splosh . . . splosh!*

More *Pteranodon* beaks slice through the ocean. *Zip . . . zap! Pteranodon* throats expand. *Glug . . . glug.* And a dozen more of your fishy friends become dactyl snacks.

I'm sad that all the dactyls are gone
now. The very last ones lived and died
at the same time as *Tyrannosaurus rex*,
65 million years ago. But every time we
dig another hollow leg or wing bone, the
dactyls still fill us with a sense of wonder.
We stop and look at the delicate fossil and
think about the ancient skies. Once they
were full of flying dragons.